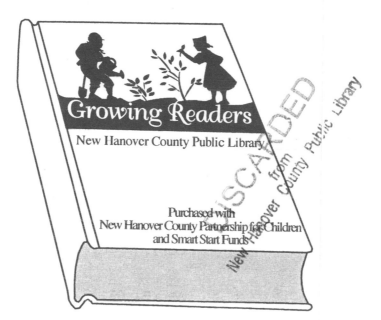

Let's Read About Our Bodies

Ears

by Cynthia Klingel* and Robert B. Noyed
photographs by Gregg Andersen

*Amoroso is preferred name

Reading consultant: Cecilia Minden-Cupp, Ph.D.,
Adjunct Professor, College of Continuing and Professional Studies, University of Virginia

For a free color catalog describing Weekly Reader® Early Learning Library's list of high-quality books, call 1-800-542-2595 or fax your request to (414) 332-3567.

Library of Congress Cataloging-in-Publication Data

Klingel, Cynthia.
    Ears / by Cynthia Klingel and Robert B. Noyed.
      p. cm. — (Let's read about our bodies)
    Includes bibliographical references and index.
    Summary: A simple introduction to ears and how they are used.
    ISBN 0-8368-3062-8 (lib. bdg.)
    ISBN 0-8368-3151-9 (softcover)
    1. Ear—Juvenile literature. 2. Hearing—Juvenile literature. [1. Ear.
2. Hearing. 3. Senses and sensation.] I. Noyed, Robert B. II. Title.
QP462.2.K575   2002
612.8'5—dc21   2001054989

This edition first published in 2002 by
Weekly Reader® Early Learning Library
330 West Olive Street, Suite 100
Milwaukee, WI 53212 USA

An Editorial Directions book
Editors: E. Russell Primm and Emily Dolbear
Art direction, design, and page production: The Design Lab
Photographer: Gregg Andersen
Weekly Reader® Early Learning Library art direction: Tammy Gruenewald
Weekly Reader® Early Learning Library production: Susan Ashley

Printed in the United States of America

1 2 3 4 5 6 7 8 9 06 05 04 03 02

Note to Educators and Parents

As a Reading Specialist I know that books for young children should engage their interest, impart useful information, and motivate them to want to learn more.

    Let's Read About Our Bodies is a new series of books designed to help children understand the value of good health and taking care of their bodies.

    A young child's active mind is engaged by the carefully chosen subjects. The imaginative text works to build young vocabularies. The short, repetitive sentences help children stay focused as they develop their own relationship with reading. The bright, colorful photographs of children enjoying good health habits complement the text with their simplicity and both entertain and encourage young children to want to learn — and read — more.

    These books are designed to be used by adults as "read-to" books to share with children to encourage early literacy in the home, school, and library. They are also suitable for more advanced young readers to enjoy on their own.

— Cecilia Minden-Cupp, Ph.D.,
    Adjunct Professor, College of Continuing and
    Professional Studies, University of Virginia

These are my ears.
I have two ears.

I have an ear
on each side
of my head.

I use my ears
to hear.

I can use my ears
to listen to songs.

I can use my
ears to listen
to my friends.

I take good care of my ears. I never put anything in my ears!

I cover my ears when noises are loud.

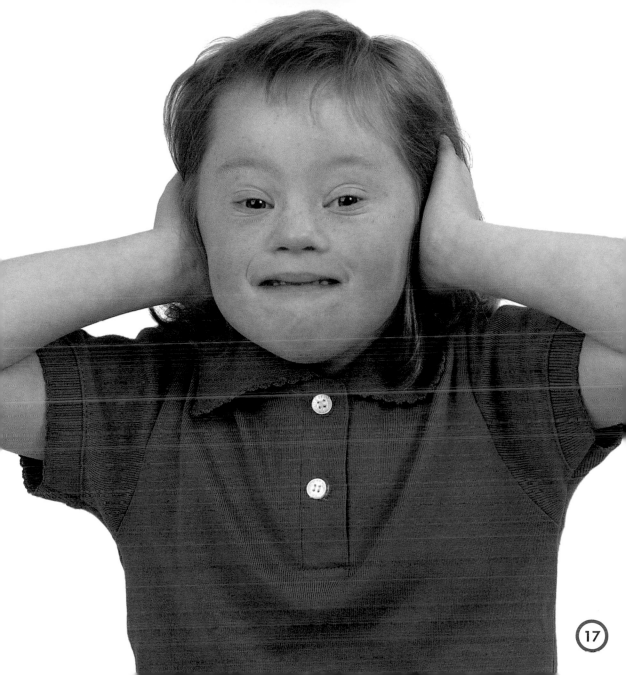

I cover my ears
with a hat when
it is cold.

Shhhh! Listen.
What can you
hear?

Glossary

hear—to sense sounds with the ear

listen—to pay attention in order to hear

noises—sounds

For More Information

Fiction Books

Dooley, Virginia. *Tubes in My Ears: My Trip to the Hospital.*
   New York: Mondo, 1996.

Perkins, Al. *The Ear Book.* New York: Random House, 1968.

Nonfiction Books

Pringle, Laurence. *Hearing.* Tarrytown, N.Y.: Benchmark
   Books, 2000.

Trumbauer, Lisa. *Animal Ears.* Mankato, Minn.:
   Pebble Books, 2000.

Web Sites

Let's Hear It for the Ear!

kidshealth.org/kid/body/ear_SW.html

For more information about the different parts of the ear

What Is Earwax?

kidshealth.org/kid/talk/yucky/earwax.html

For information about the purpose of earwax

Index

About the Authors

Cynthia Klingel has worked as a high school English teacher and an elementary school teacher. She is currently the curriculum director for a Minnesota school district. Cynthia Klingel lives with her family in Mankato, Minnesota.

Robert B. Noyed started his career as a newspaper reporter. Since then, he has worked in school communications and public relations at the state and national level. Robert B. Noyed lives with his family in Brooklyn Center, Minnesota.